S0-ADV-938

Instant Bible Lessons

God's Angels

by Pamela J. Kuhn

For information regarding the CPSIA on this printed material call:
203-595-3636 and provide reference # LANC-315751

These pages may be copied.
Permission is granted to the original buyer of this book
to photocopy student materials in this book for
use with Sunday school or Bible teaching classes.

Rainbow Publishers®

Rainbow Publishers • P.O. Box 261129 • San Diego, CA 92196
www.RainbowPublishers.com

Dedicated to . . .

Janene Beers Dubbeld, my "you can do it" friend.
And especially in memory of her namesake, Sarah Janene Kuhn.
Have fun playing with the angels, Princess!

INSTANT BIBLE LESSONS: GOD'S ANGELS
© 2011 by Rainbow Publishers, fifteenth printing
ISBN 10: 1-885358-30-X
ISBN 13: 978-1-885358-30-1
Rainbow reorder# RB36624
RELIGION / Christian Ministry / Children

Rainbow Publishers
P.O. Box 261129
San Diego, CA 92196
www.RainbowPublishers.com

Cover Illustrator: Phyllis Harris
Interior Illustrators: Joel Ryan, Roger Johnson

Certified Chain of Custody
Promoting Sustainable
Forest Management
www.sfiprogram.org

SUSTAINABLE FORESTRY INITIATIVE

Scriptures are from the *Holy Bible: New International Version* (North American Edition), copyright ©1973, 1978, 1984 by the International Bible Society. Used by permission of Zondervan Bible Publishers.

Permission is granted to the buyer of this book to photocopy student materials for use with Sunday school or Bible teaching classes.

All rights reserved. Except as noted above, no part of this publication may be reproduced, stored in a retrieval system, or transmitted in any form or by any means without written permission of Rainbow Publishers.

Printed in the United States of America

Contents

Introduction

Angels, angels everywhere you look. Books about angels, angel pins, angels on cups, even angel fabric. Are our children believing that angels are all-powerful and all-knowing? *God's Angels* is designed to teach children that God is the only one who can do all and who knows all. Angels are simply God's messengers and helpers. Their most important task is to obey God (Psalm 91:11).

God's Angels contains dozens of activities based on angels as described in the Bible. Each of the first eight chapters includes a Bible story, memory verse and numerous activities to help reinforce the truth in the lesson. An additional chapter contains miscellaneous projects that can be used anytime throughout the study. Teacher helps are also sprinkled throughout the book, including bulletin board ideas and discussion starters.

As you work through the lessons, you may use your own judgment as to the appropriateness of the projects for your class. Everything in this book is designed to meet the 5 to 10 age range, however some activities may be more appealing to a younger group while others will more readily meet the abilities of older children.

The most exciting aspect of the *Instant Bible Lessons* series, which includes *Bible Truths, Virtues and Values* and *Talking to God* as well as *God's Angels,* is its flexibility. You can easily adapt these lessons to a Sunday School hour, a children's church service, a Wednesday night Bible study or home use. And, because there is a variety of reproducible ideas from which to choose (see below), you will enjoy creating a class session that is best for your group of students—whether large or small, beginning or advanced, active or studious. Plus, the intriguing topics will keep your kids coming back for more, week after week.

With *God's Angels,* you will teach the truth about angels and your students will learn the joy of obeying God as exemplified by angels. God bless you as you use this book to show God's great love for His children. Consider yourself praised.

How to Use This Book

Each chapter begins with a Bible story which you may read to your class, followed by discussion questions. Then, use any or all of the activities in the chapter to help drive home the message of that lesson. All of the activities are tagged with one of the icons below, so you can quickly flip through the chapter and select the projects you need. Simply cut off the teacher instructions on the pages and duplicate as desired. Also, see pages 87 and 88 for reproducible notes you can fill in and send home to parents.

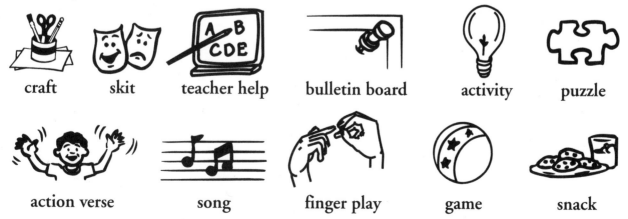

craft   skit   teacher help   bulletin board   activity   puzzle

action verse   song   finger play   game   snack

Chapter 1
God Gave Me an Angel

Memory Verse

See that you do not look down on one of these little ones. For I tell you that their angels in heaven always see the face of my Father in heaven. Matthew 18:10

Story to Share
Like a Child

The twelve disciples of Jesus were arguing among themselves. "Who do you think will be considered the most worthy in the eyes of God?" asked one.

"I think it will be Peter," said one.

"No, not Peter," argued another. "I think it will be John."

"Why don't we ask Jesus," suggested one of the disciples. "He will know."

Jesus didn't answer right away, but instead called to a child who was playing nearby. Jesus lifted the child on His lap and asked, "Do you see this child? The person that will be the greatest in Heaven will be like a child, trusting, open and humble. And the one who loves a child and teaches him or her about Me, they are to be praised."

The disciples didn't know what to say. They had no idea that children were so important to Jesus.

Jesus smiled and hugged the child on His lap. "Make sure you don't look down on these little ones. They have angels in heaven that stand by the throne of my Father, waiting to help the children when God commands."

Looking straight at His disciples Jesus said, "The children should be loved and cared for in the same way a shepherd loves and cares for his sheep. A good shepherd will search all night to find a lost lamb because it is precious to him. Every child is precious to God." Then he reached out to the rest of the children who had gathered, and blessed them.

— based on Matthew 18:1-14

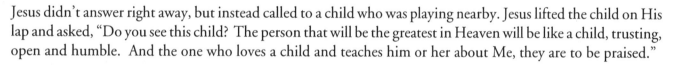

Questions for Discussion

1. Would you have liked to sit on Jesus' lap? What would you have said to Him?
2. Did you know you have an angel that is ready to take care of you when God sees you need help?

puzzle

God Gave Angels for All

Materials
- puzzle, duplicated to heavy white paper
- crayons
- scissors
- envelopes

Directions
1. Have the class color and cut out the puzzle. They should cut the puzzle apart on the solid lines.
2. Allow the children to decorate an envelope to store the pieces in.
3. Say, **Play with this puzzle at home with your friends so they can know about Jesus, too.**

See that you do not look down on one of these little ones.

For I tell you that their angels in heaven always see the face of my Father in heaven.

Matthew 18:10

God's Gift to Me

Matthew 18:10

Materials

- gift and angel, duplicated
- crayons
- scissors
- paper fasteners

Directions

1. Have the class color and cut out the gift and the angel.
2. Show how to use a paper fastener to attach the angel to the gift.
3. Demonstrate how to move the angel from behind to pop up from the gift.

Discuss

Say, **God loves you so much that He gave you a special gift.** He gave you an angel who stands in the presence of God. What other gifts has God given you?

God Gave Me an Angel

My Angel

song

Directions

Sing to the tune of "Standing in the Need of Prayer."

Usage

This is an ideal way to quiet the children before prayer. If your class is mostly of reading-age, photocopy the song so they can more easily join in.

I have, I have an angel,
Standing in the presence of God.
I have, I have an angel,
Standing in the presence of God.

It's not my mother's, not my father's,
but it's mine, all mine,
Standing in the presence of God.
It's not my brother's, not my sister's,
But it's mine, all mine,
Standing in the presence of God.

You have, You have an angel,
Standing in the presence of God.
You have, You have an angel,
Standing in the presence of God.

It's not your mother's, not your father's,
but it's yours, my friend,
Standing in the presence of God.
It's not your brother's, not your sister's,
But it's yours, my friend,
Standing in the presence of God.

God Gave Me an Angel

Angel Cut-Out

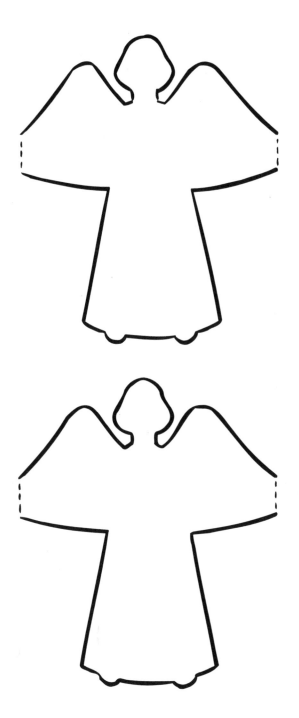

craft

Materials
- colored paper or pages from wall-paper books
- scissors
- crayons or glitter glue pens

Directions
1. Show how to fold an 8½" x 11" horizontal piece of paper into fourths, accordian style.
2. Have the children trace the angel patterns onto the top fold, making sure the angel wings are placed at the edges.
3. Show how to cut out the angels, making sure to not cut on the dashed line edges of the wings.
4. Allow the class to color around the edges of the angels with a crayon or glitter glue pen.
5. Tell the students to write their names and their friends' names on each angel.

God Gave Me an Angel

Thank You, God

Usage

Younger children especially enjoy action rhymes — a quick cure for "the fidgets." Direct the class to an open area with space to move around, if possible. Demonstrate the rhyme first, then repeat it several times. You will be surprised how quickly the class catches on!

God gave me an angel.

> *point to self*

God gave you an angel, too.

> *point to a friend*

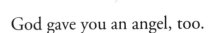

Our angels are in heaven,

> *point to the sky*

Higher than the twinkly stars

> *wiggle fingers over head*

Thank you, God, for my angel,

> *fold hands in prayer*

You gave to watch over me.

> *point to sky, then to self*

Memory Verse Rebus

Figure out the memory verse by writing the word represented by the picture or bold letters on the line. Here is an example:

= see

Now, if you can do the rest by yourself. After you finish the puzzle, practice memorizing the verse.

 that **U** do not look down on **1** of

these . **4** I tell **U** that their

in (castle image) always  the face

of my Father in (castle image) . Matthew 18:10

Solution is on page 96.

_____ that _____ do not look down on _____

of these _____ . _____ I tell _____

that their _____ in _____

always _____ the face of my Father in _____ .

Matthew 18:10

puzzle

· · · · · · · · · · · ·

Materials

- puzzle, duplicated
- pencils
- Bibles

Directions

1. Have the students fill in the blanks with the correct words as shown in the pictures.
2. Help them memorize the Bible verse.

Usage

Puzzles are a fun way to teach memory verses. You may use this puzzle with "Missing Es and Os" on page 14 to gently impress this lesson's verse on your class.

God Gave Me an Angel

Missing Os and Es

All of the Os and Es are missing from our memory verse! Insert an E or an O in each blank, then read the completed memory verse. Can you memorize it? Give your paper to a friend and recite the verse, then trade places and let your friend recite the verse.

Materials
• puzzle, duplicated
• pencils
• Bibles

Directions
1. Have the children fill in the blanks with the correct letters.
2. Help them to memorize the verse.

Usage

Puzzles create quiet work time for students. Make yourself available to those who need assistance, but encourage the children to work alone in solving the puzzle to gain the most benefits.

S___ ___ that y___u d___ n___t l___ ___k

d___wn ___n ___n___ ___f th___s___ littl___

___n___s. F___r I t___ll y___u that th___ir

ang___ls in h___av___n always s___ ___ th___

fac___ ___f my Fath___r in h___av___n.

Matth___w 18:10

Solution is on page 96.

Angelic Bulletin Board

bulletin board

. . . .

Materials
- wings and tag, duplicated
- lollipops
- white fabric or tissue paper
- yarn
- scissors
- blue and gold paper

Directions
1. Cover the bulletin board with blue paper.
2. Cut one 6" circle from fabric for each child.
3. Wrap the circle around the candy top and tie at the base with yarn.
4. Cut out the wings and glue to the backs of the lollipops.
5. Cut out the tags, write each child's name on one and tie to the yarn.
6. Attach the candy to the board with push pins.
7. Cut "An Angel for Me" lettering from gold paper.
8. Post cotton on the base of the angels.
9. Cut stars from gold paper to fill in empty spaces.

God Gave Me an Angel

An Angel for Me

_____

See that you do not look down on one of these little ones. For I tell you that their angels in heaven always see the face of my Father in heaven. Matthew 18:10

An Angel for Me

_____

See that you do not look down on one of these little ones. For I tell you that their angels in heaven always see the face of my Father in heaven. Matthew 18:10

15

Chapter 2
My Angel Rejoices With Me

Memory Verse

For God so loved the world that he gave his one and only Son, that whoever believes in him shall not perish but have eternal life. John 3:16

Story to Share
A Savior Is Born

One glorious night, Jesus was born in Bethlehem. The Savior everyone was praying and hoping for had come to earth as a tiny baby. He was born in a stable, where animals were kept. His bed was a manger.

Shepherds were watching their sheep in the hills near Bethlehem. The night was dark. Suddenly there was a brilliant light that pierced through the darkness. In the midst of the light stood an angel.

The shepherds were frightened. "What was the great light?" they asked each other as they huddled together.

The angel said to them, "Don't be afraid. I have a message full of joy for you. A Savior was born tonight in Bethlehem."

Just then there was a sky full of angels. They were rejoicing with the angel. A Savior was born! "Glory to God in the highest," they were singing.

When the rejoicing angels went back to heaven the shepherds wanted to go see their Savior. This was the One, sent from God, who would be able to save the shepherds—and us—from sin. But first, Jesus had to be offered as a spotless, sinless sacrifice to pay the penalty for our sins. He willingly died for us, so that our hearts could be clean.

Our only duty is to ask Jesus to forgive us of our sins (those things we know we shouldn't have done). When we do, the rejoicing angels join in praise with all heaven. They know that with a clean heart we'll someday live with them in heaven.

Only Jesus can forgive our sins. Angels cannot, but they do rejoice when we ask Jesus to forgive our sins. There is more rejoicing in heaven over one sinner that asks forgiveness than over 99 that have already been forgiven.

— based on Luke 2:8-20

Questions for Discussion

1. Have you asked Jesus to forgive you of your sins?
2. If you did, angels rejoiced in heaven. If you haven't, would you like to now?

A Clean Heart

craft

Materials

- heart, duplicated to heavy white paper
- head, hands and feet, duplicated to light pink paper
- crayons
- scissors
- glue
- wiggly eyes
- yarn
- hole punch

Directions

1. Have the children cut out the heart, head, hands and feet.
2. Allow them to color the hair and lips.
3. Show how to add wiggle eyes to the face.
4. Instruct the class to punch holes at the dots on the figure.
5. Let the children cut yarn. Help them tie the body pieces to the heart. Tie on an extra length of yarn for hanging at the top outer dots.

My Angel Rejoices With Me

My angel rejoices when my heart is clean!

Luke 15:7

Hiding Angels

How many angels can you find in the picture below?

puzzle

Suddenly a great company of the heavenly host appeared with the angel, praising God and saying, "Glory to God in the highest, and on earth peace to men on whom his favor rests." Luke 2:13-14

Solution is on page 96.

Materials
•puzzle, duplicated
•pencils

Usage
Even the youngest children in your group will be able to work on this word-less puzzle. Have copies ready for early birds to begin working while others arrive.

My Angel Rejoices With Me

Rejoicing With Angels

craft/song

• • • • • • • • • • • • •

Materials

- angel finger puppet, duplicated
- crayons
- scissors
- tape

Directions

1. Have the students color and cut out the finger puppet. You may copy more than one angel per student.
2. Show how to wrap the paper strip around your fingers and tape to secure.
3. The students may use their puppets to sing the song. Have them hold their hands on their laps until the chorus, then pop up and wiggle their fingers for "angels rejoiced."
4. Sing the song to the tune of "Jesus Loves Me."

My Angel Rejoices
With Me

Jesus was born in Bethlehem.
Angels rejoiced that the Savior came.
Shepherds listened to their song,
As they gave God their acclaim.

Angels rejoiced,
Angels rejoiced,
Angels rejoiced,
A Savior came to earth.

When my heart is black with sin,
And I need to be forgiv'n.
Jesus washes my heart clean.
Angels rejoice again in heav'n.

Angels rejoice,
Angels rejoice,
Angels rejoice,
When Jesus makes me clean.

My Angel
Rejoices
With Me.

Window Angels

Materials
•angel, duplicated
•potato peelers
•old crayons
•waxed paper
•string
•iron
•hole punch

Directions
1. Have the class cut out two angels on outer lines, then show how to cut out the center to make two frames.
2. Using peelers, have the students shave crayons onto pieces of waxed paper.
3. Cover their shavings with another piece of waxed paper. Iron the two together, using low heat and no steam.
4. The students should then trace the outside of the angel frame onto the ironed waxed paper and cut out.
5. The waxed paper angel may then be glued between the two angel frames.
6. Punch a hole at the top of the angels, and tie on string for hanging.

My Angel Rejoices With Me

Heaven Rejoices!

Write the missing words in the puzzle below.
Then look up Luke 15:7 to check your work.

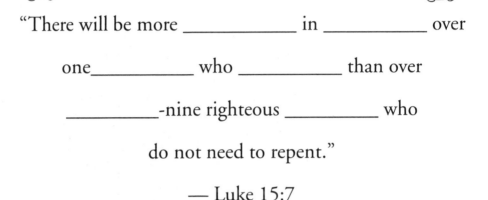

Materials

•puzzle, duplicated
•pencils

"There will be more _____ in _____ over

one_____ who _____ than over

_____-nine righteous _____ who

do not need to repent."

— Luke 15:7

Usage

This puzzle may be more of a challenge for younger children. To help them, you may insert numbers on the puzzle and in the corresponding blanks.

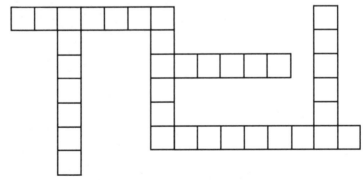

Solution is on page 96.

My Angel Rejoices With Me

22

Little Angels Finger Play

One little angel came to share the news,

With the quiet shepherds watching o'er their lambs.

"Don't be afraid," she told the frightened men,

"A Savior is born in Bethlehem."

Suddenly the heavens

Were filled with shining light.

A multitude of angels

Sang to them that night.

"Jesus is born,"

The angels did sing.

Glory, hallelujah!

Joy to you we bring.

Directions

Hold up one finger and wiggle it, moving your hand back and forth until you say, "the heavens were filled," then hold up all 10 and wiggle them until the end of the poem.

My Angel Rejoices With Me

23

A Surprise Word

Using the pictures as clues, fill in the letters to see who will rejoice
when your heart is clean.

Materials
•puzzle, duplicated
•pencils

Usage
Instruct the children to wait until everyone has finished before discussing the answers. Help younger students with spelling, possibly leading the whole class together (if you have mostly young students) as they solve the puzzle.

H _ R P

WI _ G S

S I N _

H _ A V E N

H A _ O

T R U M P E T_

_ _ _ _ _ _   REJOICE!

Solution is on page 96.

Star Pupils

Who was Jesus' mother?

Who was Jesus' earthly father?

Where was Jesus born?

Who were watching their sheep?

Who came to tell the shepherds that Jesus was born?

What do angels do when our sins are forgiven?

Joseph

shepherds

in a stable

rejoice

Mary

angels

puzzle

Materials

- stars and angels, duplicated
- glue
- scissors

Directions

1. Have the students cut out the stars.
2. They should read the questions on the angels, then glue the star with the correct answer to each angel.
3. After everyone is finished, review the questions and answers.

My Angel Rejoices With Me

Solution is on page 96.

Chapter 3
My Angel Guides Me

Memory Verse

Praise the Lord, you his angels, you mighty ones who do his bidding, who obey his word. Psalm 103:20

Story to Share
Peter, Get Up

King Herod Agrippa was angry at the apostles. Every day the apostles would gather at one of the temple gates and talk about Jesus. The king didn't like his people becoming followers of Christ.

Already the king had executed Christians, and now he arrested Peter and threw him into prison. Soldiers were watching Peter at all times. He was chained to two of them, while others watched the door.

One night Peter was sleeping. Suddenly he was awakened out of his sleep. Something had struck him on his side! Looking up, Peter saw an angel in a blaze of light.

"Get up quickly," the angel said. "Put on your cloak and sandals and follow me."

Peter obeyed, and as he sat up his chains fell off. Following the angel, he wondered if he was dreaming. Surely it wasn't real! They passed the guards at the door. The prison doors opened without anyone touching them. Once they were out in the street, the guiding angel disappeared. Peter knew then that he wasn't dreaming, but that God had sent the angel to guide him from prison and away from King Herod.

Peter didn't waste any time. He went straight to the home of Mary, mother of Mark. A number of people were there praying for his safety. Rhoda, a young servant girl, heard his knock. When she came to the door and saw Peter she was so excited that, instead of inviting him in, she ran back and told the group that Peter was there.

"You are seeing things," the people said. "It cannot be him; he is in prison. It must be his angel."

"No, it is Peter at the door. I saw him!" insisted Rhoda.

"Maybe it is his ghost," one of them said.

"I can still hear someone knocking," another replied. "We should go open the door."

The group was surprised to see that it really was Peter. They praised God for sending an angel to guide him.

— based on Acts 12:5-17

Questions for Discussion

1. You probably haven't ever been in prison, but have you been lost? How did it feel?
2. Did you pray for God to help you find your way?

Peter's Guiding Angel

song

Directions

Sing to the tune of "Reuben, Reuben, I've Been Thinking." If your class has good reading skills, photocopy the song and allow them to read along and join in.

Peter, Peter, there in prison,
Not deserving to be there.
God has not forgotten you;
Prayers are prayed by those who care.

Peter, Peter, as you sleep,
In the prison oh, so late.
A quiet angel comes to wake you;
Guides you through those iron gates.

Peter, Peter, as you're knocking,
On Mary's door while they pray.
They don't believe the servant, Rhoda,
"It just can't be who you say."

Peter, Peter, keep on knocking,
Soon they will open wide the door.
They will know your little secret—
Don't worry, just trust God some more.

Peter, Peter, God sent an angel,
To deliver you that night.
He will always come to help us,
With His help we'll do what's right.

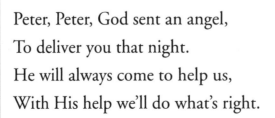

The Most Important Thing

puzzle

There is one thing angels do that makes them very special.
And it's something we can do, too.
Using the graph, fill in the letters below to find out what it is.

	1	2	3	4	5	6	7
A	Y	H	A	D	B	O	R
B	O	E	O	N	A	T	L
C	B	U	G	A	G	W	E
D	N	O	E	O	N	A	T
E	I	H	A	D	S	O	R

__ __ __ __ __ __   __ __ __ __
E3 D5 C5 C7 B7 E5   D4 C1 B2 A1

__ __ __ .
C3 A6 E4

Solution is on page 96.

Materials
•puzzle, duplicated
•pencils

Usage

This puzzle concept may be new to your class, so take some time to explain how it works. You may also use this graph to create your own puzzles.

My Angel Guides Me

Peter and the Guiding Angel

skit

• • • • • • • • • • • •

Materials
•yarn
•hole punch

Directions
Before beginning the skit, read Acts 12:5-17 to the class. If the children are not yet able to read the script, they may repeat the lines after you or act out the parts as you narrate. Let the children take turns playing the angel and Peter. Cut out the card at right, punch holes at the dots and use yarn to tie it around the angel's neck.

Peter:	*lies with paper chains on hands, sleeping*
Angel:	*strikes Peter on the side*
	Peter, come quickly.
Peter:	*sits up, breaks chains off*
Angel:	Put on your sandals and cloak.
Peter:	*puts on shoes and wraps coat around himself*
	Am I dreaming?
Angel:	*disappears*
Peter:	I am not dreaming. An angel guided me out of prison.
All:	*kneeling in prayer*
	God rescue Peter.
Peter:	*knocks on door*
Rhoda:	Peter! It is Peter!
All:	It cannot be.
Rhoda:	It is Peter.
All:	God has rescued Peter. Praise God for His guiding angel.

The Guiding Angel

Angels Obediently Guide Us

Praise the Lord, you his angels, you mighty ones who do his bidding, who obey his word. Psalm 103:20

action verse

• • • • • • • • • • •

Praise the Lord,

raise hands in praise

You his angels.

move arms up and down at sides as if moving wings

You mighty ones who do his bidding,

flex arms to show muscles

Who obey his words.

shake forefinger

Usage

Is your class having trouble paying attention to the lesson? Have them all stand and lead them in this quick action verse. Repeat it together until everyone has it memorized!

My Angel Guides Me

31

puzzle

Materials
•puzzle, duplicated
•pencils

Usage
Kids of all ages like mazes! Have the maze copied and ready for early arrivals or as a filler for those extra minutes at the end of your session.

Standing Guard

King Herod was determined that Peter would not escape.
He had Peter's hands chained to one guard and his feet to another.
Others were at the door to make sure he didn't escape.
Be an angel and help Peter find his way past the guards and
through the streets to Mary's home.

*Praise the Lord, you his angels, you mighty
ones who do his bidding, who obey his word.*
Psalm 103:20

Solution is on page 96.

**My Angel
Guides Me**

Broken Chains

Use the words on the chain below
to answer the following questions.

1. What security measures were taken to keep Peter in the prison? _____

2. What was Peter doing when the angel came? _____

3. How did the angel wake him up? _____

4. How did they get through the iron gate leading to the city? _____

5. Where did Peter go when the angel left him? _____

6. What were they doing there? _____

7. Who came to the door? _____

8. Did they believe it was Peter? _____

9. What was the believer's reaction when they saw Peter? _____

10. What is your lesson from this story? _____

Materials
• puzzle, duplicated
• pencils

Directions

Using the words on the chains, have the students fill in the blanks to answer the questions. Suggest that they turn to Acts 12:5-17 if they need help.

Discuss

Say, **God sent an angel to guide Peter out of the prison at night. Can you imagine what it must have been like when everyone awoke and found him gone?**

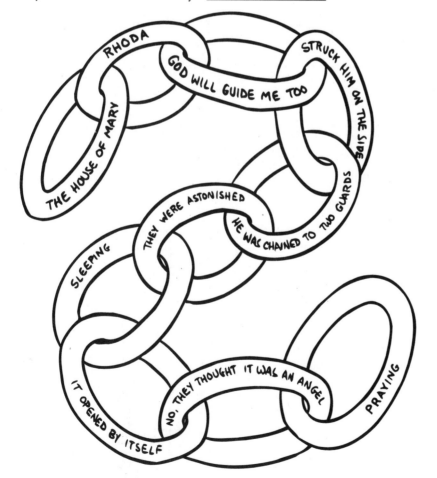

Solution is on page 96.

My Angel Guides Me

33

craft

Materials

- picture boxes, duplicated
- crayons
- glue
- craft sticks, six per child

Directions

1. Have the children color and cut out the story pictures.
2. Show how to glue the pictures to the tops of craft sticks.
3. Allow the students to hold up the correct picture as you tell the story. Older children may take turns reading the story as the rest of the class holds up their stick pictures.
4. Encourage the children to tell the story to friends and family using the sticks at home.

Stick Story

Story

1. Peter was in prison for preaching about Jesus.
2. Faithful Christians were praying for him.
3. An angel came at night to guide him out of prison.
4. Peter knocked on the door where the people were praying.
5. The people praised God for answering their prayers.
6. God will always help me if I trust Him.

Ten Little Angels

One little, two little,
Three little angels.
Four little, five little,
Six little angels.
Seven little, eight little,
Nine little angels.
Ten little angels obeying God.

I will, I will,
I will obey God.
I will, I will,
I will obey God.
I will, I will,
I will obey God.
I will obey God, too.

song

. . . .

Directions
Sing to the tune of "Ten Little Indians." Lead everyone in holding up fingers for the number of angels in each phrase of the first verse.

My Angel Guides Me

35

Chapter 4

My Angel Protects Me

Memory Verse

The Lord delivers him in times of trouble. Psalm 41:1

Story to Share
God Sends a Protecting Angel

"Be it known that any man who makes any request of any god or man except the king will be thrown into the den of lions." This was the decree that was read all over King Darius' kingdom.

King Darius had been tricked into making this wicked law by men who were jealous of Daniel, one of the king's most trusted men.

"If we get the king to make this law, Daniel is dead!" exclaimed one wicked man. "He always prays to that God of his."

"That's right," said another wicked man. "And we can't catch him lying or cheating or doing anything wrong. He always does what is right." So they tricked the king and the law was made.

Daniel heard about the wicked law, but he would not obey any order that would cause him to give honor to a man when it belonged to God. Knowing that praying would mean the lions would soon be having him for lunch, Daniel knelt at his window, which was in full view of the street, to thank God for his blessings and to ask God to bless his people.

"Come, let's report him to the king," said the wicked men, rubbing their hands together with joy.

As soon as Daniel's deed had been told, King Darius knew he had been tricked. But a law could not be changed, so the king gave the order for Daniel to be thrown into the den of lions. "I'm sorry, Daniel," he said. "Your God will protect you."

Daniel was thrown into the den of roaring, hungry lions. But before his feet touched the rocks, God sent an angel to protect Daniel.

Early the next morning, the king came to the door of the den. "Daniel, Daniel. Did your God protect you?"

"Yes, my king," Daniel answered. "God sent His angel to close the mouths of the lions. I am unharmed."

King Darius was overjoyed. He gave the order for Daniel to be released from the lions' den. A new decree was made. "Everyone in my kingdom shall respect the God of Daniel. He is the living God."

— based on Daniel 6:1-28

Questions for Discussion

1. What are you afraid of?
2. What does Psalm 41:1-2 say about being in scary places?

Bible Verse Protection

Use your Bible to look up the verses on the bottom of the page.
Then fill in the missing words on the lines.

```
_ _ _ _ _ _ P _
_ _ _ _ _ _ R _
       _ O _ _ _ _
   _ _ _ _ T _ _
 _ _ _ _ E
     _ _ _ C _ _ _
       _ _ _'T
_ _ _ _ _ _ _ I _ _
 _ _ _ _ _ O _ _
         N _ _ _ _ _ _
```

Materials
•puzzle, duplicated
•pencils
•Bibles

Usage
This is an absorbing puzzle for your older class members. Be sure everyone has a Bible in which to look up the verses. You may need to assist younger students in finding the verses in their Bibles.

1. Psalm 34:7 — "The angel of the Lord _____ around those who fear him, and he delivers them."

2. Psalm 91:4 — "He will cover you with his _____, and under his wings you will find refuge."

3. Daniel 6:22 — "My God sent his angel, and he shut the _____ of the lions."

4. Isaiah 25:4 — "You have been…a _____ from the storm."

5. Psalm 125:2 — "As the mountains surround Jerusalem, so the Lord surrounds his _____ both now and forevermore."

6. Psalm 17:6 — "I _____ on you, O God, for you will answer me."

7. 2 Kings 6:16 — "_____ be afraid,…Those who are with us are more than those who are with them."

8. Psalm 91:11 — "For he will command his angels _____ you to guard you in all your ways."

9. Matthew 10:31 — "So don't be afraid; you are worth more than many _____."

10. Matthew 10:30 — "And even the very hairs of your head are all _____."

Solution is on page 96.

Light Switch Reminder

craft

. . . .

Materials
- light switch covers, duplicated to heavy white paper
- "glow-in-the-dark" paint
- paint brushes
- newspaper
- paint smocks
- scissors

Directions
1. Have the children cut out the light switch covers. They may need adult assistance to cut out the centers.
2. Place newspaper on the table to be used for painting. Provide smocks or large shirts to cover the children's clothing while they paint the light switch covers.
3. Tell the students how to hang the cover at home. Say, **Each night you turn out your light, your angel will remind you of God's protection.**

MY ANGEL

PROTECTS ME

MY ANGEL

PROTECTS ME

My Angel Protects Me

· · · · · · · · · · · · ·

Materials
• page, duplicated
• pencils

Directions

1. Discuss fears with the class. Name some things of which children are often afraid and ask them to name some of their own.
2. Pass out the duplicated sheets and pencils.
3. After the children have completed their prayers, ask for volunteers to read theirs.
4. Close with prayer for all fears and thank God for His protection and help.

My Angel Protects Me

We Have Lions, Too

What are you afraid of?
Do you have lions' mouths that you need closed?
On the lions below write your fears.
Then write your prayer to God,
asking for His protection and help.

Dear God,

I am afraid of _____

_____

_____

_____

_____

Amen

Lion Check-Up

The Lord

delivers him

in times

of trouble.

The Lord

will protect him

and preserve

his life.

Psalm 41:1-2

activity

. . . .

Materials
• rock pattern and lions, duplicated
• construction paper
• glue

Directions

1. Have the students use the rock pattern to cut out nine rocks from construction paper.

2. Show how to glue the rocks over the words on each lion, just at the top of the rock so it may be flipped up and read.

3. As the children recite the memory verse, they may lift up a rock to check their work.

My Angel Protects Me

Afraid? Trust in God

Psalm 56:3 tells us what we can do when we are afraid.
Unscramble the words below to find out the answer.

——— I am ———, I ——— ——— ———
hewn   rafadi   ilwl   ustrt

in ———.
uyo

Materials
•puzzle, duplicated
•pencils
•crayons

Usage
This is a quick puzzle to use as a time-filler. You may also allow the children to color the picture of the lion.

God will protect us from danger!

Solution is on page 96.

**My Angel
Protects Me**

Rrrr-oar!

1. "Rrrr-oar," said the lions as
   they waited for their meal.
   "Rrrr-oar, Rrrr-oar, Rrrr-oar,"
   they could not be still.

2. "Throw him to the lions,"
   the wicked men did say.
   Daniel did nothing wrong;
   all he did was pray.

3. God knew what was happening;
   He sent an angel there.
   And all the lions' mouths were
   closed; they didn't hurt a hair.

4. Whenever I am scared,
   of grrr-owls, and rrrr-oars, and
   boos,
   My God will send my angel,
   and I'll be protected, too.

action verse

. . . .

Directions

Split the class into two groups, then select one student to be the angel and another to be Daniel. Have the students do the following actions (coordinated with numbered verses) as you read the poem:

1. First group growls, imitating lions.
2. Second group points to lions while Daniel kneels and prays.
3. Angel walks into den and lions are quiet.
4. Everyone growls, roars and boos, then is quiet for last line as they point to heaven and hug themselves.

Repeat the action rhyme several times so everyone may have a chance to play the parts.

My Angel Protects Me

Lots of Lions

bulletin board

Materials
- Daniel and lion (p. 45) patterns
- clear, self-stick plastic
- double-sided tape
- construction paper
- scissors
- markers

Directions
1. Post gray paper on the board with lettering that says, "I am protected because I know God."
2. Duplicate 12 lions.
3. Write the questions from p. 45 on the front and the answers on the back of the lions. Cover with clear, self-stick plastic. Place tape or Velcro on the backs.
4. Cut out the Daniel figure.
5. Place Daniel on one side of the board and the lions on the other.
6. The children may pull the lions off of the board. If their answer is correct they may move the lion next to Daniel.
7. For a game, write point values on the backs of the lions.

My Angel Protects Ms

44

Questions

1. What decree was read all over King Darius' kingdom?
2. Why did King Darius make this wicked law?
3. How many times per day did Daniel kneel to pray?
4. Where did Daniel kneel to pray?
5. Did Daniel know about the law forbidding prayer?
6. Did Daniel hide to pray, afraid he would be thrown into the den of lions?
7. Could a law be changed once it was made?
8. Were the lions hungry?
9. Who did God send to protect Daniel?
10. Was King Darius happy that God protected Daniel?
11. What new decree was given?
12. What happened to the men who had tricked the king?

Answers

1. Be it known that any man who makes any request of any god or man except the king for 30 days will be thrown into the den of lions.
2. Men who were jealous of Daniel had tricked him into it.
3. three times
4. near a window facing Jerusalem
5. yes
6. no
7. no
8. yes
9. an angel
10. yes
11. Everyone in my kingdom shall respect the God of Daniel. He is the living God.
12. They were thrown into the lions' den.

Reference — Daniel 6:1-28

Chapter 5

My Angel Cares for Me

Memory Verse

I am with you and will watch over you wherever you go. Genesis 28:15

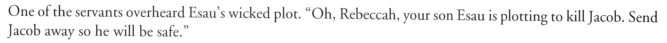

Story to Share

A Stairway of Angels

Esau was holding a grudge against his twin brother, Jacob. Jacob had received the blessing from his father, Isaac, a blessing which belonged to Esau because he was the eldest.

"I hate that brother of mine," murmured Esau with gritted teeth. "My father is old and will die soon. Then I am going to kill my brother."

One of the servants overheard Esau's wicked plot. "Oh, Rebeccah, your son Esau is plotting to kill Jacob. Send Jacob away so he will be safe."

Rebeccah called Jacob to her. "Quick, Jacob, you must leave. Esau is planning to kill you. Go to my brother Laban in Haran, and stay there until Esau's anger cools."

So Jacob started out on his long journey. Day after day he walked. His feet became tired and sore. He felt sad and alone, like no one cared for him. One evening, tired from walking, Jacob stopped for the night. He lay down on the ground to sleep, placing a large stone under his head for a pillow.

He dreamed he saw a stairway set on earth and reaching up to heaven. Angels were moving up and down the ladder and at the top of the great stairway stood God. "I am with you and will keep you everywhere you go, and will bring you again to this land," said God.

When Jacob awoke early the next morning, he was filled with comfort. God was with him! God cared for him! "This is an awesome place; surely God was with me and I did not know it."

Jacob took the stone he had used for a pillow and stood it upright. Pouring oil over the stone as a reminder of God's presence, he said, "This place shall be called Bethel," which means "house of God."

As Jacob went on his journey, he remembered God's wonderful promise: "I am with you and will watch over you wherever you go." He was no longer sad or lonely. God cared for him and was with him. God would be with him wherever he went!

— based on Genesis 27:41-45; 28:10-22

Questions for Discussion

1. Have you ever had to move to another town or state?
2. How did it feel to leave your friends and to go where you didn't know anyone?

Jacob's Pillow

craft

Materials
- angel pattern, duplicated
- smooth rocks
- poster paints
- clear nail polish
- paint smocks

Directions
1. Have the class cut out the angel pattern.
2. Show how to trace the pattern onto the rock.
3. Allow the children to paint the rock angel with poster paints.
4. Let the rocks dry completely.
5. Show how to brush clear nail polish on the painted rocks to make them shine.

Discuss
Say, **Jacob used a rock for a pillow. Have you ever tried that? After he woke up, he used it for an altar. This angel rock will remind you of Jacob and God's promise that He will always care for you.**

My Angel Cares for Me

48

God Cares for Me

Jacob had to run away,
From his angry brother.
God sent angels while he slept,
And promised care forever.

It doesn't matter where I go,
Or what I have need of.
God in heav'n sends my angel,
To care for me with love.

I am with you and will watch over you wherever you go.
Genesis 28:15

My Angel Cares for Me

49

craft

Materials

- angel pattern, duplicated
- crayons
- scissors
- drinking straws

Directions

1. Have the class color and cut out the angel.
2. Show how to carefully cut the slits.
3. Allow the children to insert a straw in the slits.
4. Say, **Everytime you take a drink, repeat your memory verse.**
5. If desired, provide a beverage and cups large enough for straws so the students may try their Sippin' Angels.

My Angel Cares for Me

Sippin' Verse Angel

I am with you and will watch over you wherever you go.
Genesis 28:15

Verse Rocks

I

a m

with

you

and

will

watch

over

you

wherever

you

go.

Genesis 28:15

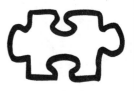
Materials

- rocks and angel, duplicated
- crayons
- scissors
- glue
- envelopes

Directions

1. Have the students cut out the rocks and the angel. You may want them to glue the page to construction paper first for durability.
2. The students may color the angel and glue it to the front of the envelope.
3. Challenge them to mix up the rocks then place them in order according to the memory verse. For a game, time them and offer a small prize to the winner.
4. Encourage the students to keep the rocks in the envelope so they can play again at home.

My Angel Cares for Me

activity

Materials

- paper bags
- newspapers
- glue or staples
- markers

Directions

1. Have the students assist you in filling the paper bags with crumpled newspaper.
2. Show how to fold the top of the bag down and glue or staple together.
3. Let the students squeeze the bags into rock shapes.
4. Read Genesis 28:11-22 as the children "sleep" on their rocks.
5. Set the rocks up and have them help you write BETHEL on them, one letter per rock, as shown at right.

Paper Bag Rocks

A Pillow?

Using the chart, color the picture below to find out what Jacob used for his pillow.

1 BLUE   **3** RED   **5** ORANGE
2 GREEN   **4** YELLOW   **6** PURPLE

puzzle

• • • • • • • • • • • •

Materials
•puzzle, duplicated
•crayons or markers

Usage
Be sure to have a good supply of the needed crayon or marker colors. An alternative way to present the puzzle is to photocopy it to overhead transparency sheets. When colored with markers, the transparencies make bright stained glass hangers.

My Angel Cares for Me

Jacob's Finger Play

Usage

Teach the motions for the rhyme, then repeat it several times so the students may learn it well. Ask, **Who is the "I" in this rhyme?** (Jacob!)

I was so, so tired as I ran away that day.

It didn't even matter on a rock my head did lay.

fold hands and lay head on them

Suddenly there were angels moving up and down the stairs.

God stood at the very top, promising me His care.

"walk" fingers up and down arm

Now I want to tell you, God will care for you.

For He loves you, and you, and you, and me, too!

point to three friends and to self

Angel Chains

craft

Materials
- angels and chain, duplicated
- crayons
- scissors
- glue

Directions

1. Duplicate the angels at least twice for each child.
2. Have the class color and cut out the angels and chain strips.
3. Show how to cut two slits in each angel.
4. Demonstrate how to loop the strips through the slits of two angels. Glue the ends of the strips together, chaining the angels to one another.
5. Hang the chains around your classroom or bulletin board, or allow the students to take their chains home to decorate their bedrooms.

GOD
CARES
FOR
ME

My Angel Cares for Me

Chapter 6
My Angel Provides for Me

Memory Verse

Put [your] hope in God, who richly provides us with everything for our enjoyment. 1 Timothy 6:17

Story to Share
Fed by Angels

Jezebel, King Ahab's wife, worshipped a false god, Baal, instead of the true God. Jezebel was angry with God's prophet Elijah, who had made a mockery of Baal by proving he could not hear the prayers of his worshippers. And then he had ordered the execution of the prophets of Baal. Jezebel was seeking revenge.

"I hate him,"screamed Jezebel. "May the gods kill me if I do not take his life within 24 hours. Take that message to Elijah."

Elijah was frightened when he heard the message. "Quick, servant, we must depart. Let's go to the kingdom of Jehoshaphat," he said, hurriedly. "We will be safe there."

Running for his life, Elijah continued until he reached Beersheba and knew he was safe. "You stay here," he told his servant. "I am going on into the wilderness to be alone and to pray."

Elijah went a day's journey into the wilderness. He was very tired from his trip. He sat down under a juniper tree and prayed, "I'm so tired, Lord. I've had enough; just let me die." And with those words he fell asleep.

Soon he was awakened. When he looked to see who had touched him, he saw an angel. The angel said, "God sent me to provide for you. Arise and eat." Elijah looked and there was a cake and a jar of water. It tasted so good to Elijah but, still tired from his journey, he slept again.

The angel of the Lord obediently watched over Elijah while he slept. When it was again time to eat, the angel woke him. "You are tired from your journey, but you need to eat,"said the angel.

Elijah drank the water and ate the food the angel provided. What special food the angel fed him! With the strength from that food, Elijah traveled 40 days and nights to Horeb.

— based on 1 Kings 19:1-9

Questions for Discussion

1. What do you need? (food, clothes, shelter, etc.)
2. Do you have these things? God always provides what we need!

craft

Materials
•stars, duplicated
•9" paper plates
•glue
•glitter
•scissors

Directions
1. Show how to cut out the center of a paper plate.
2. Have the students spread a thin layer of glue on one side of the plate, then sprinkle glitter on it.
3. Allow the class to color the stars at right, cut them out and glue them to the top of the halo.
4. Say, **Wear your halo so you can remember to be an angel.**

Discuss
Say, **Sometimes we say someone is a little angel, which is another way of saying that person is really well-behaved. What are some ways you can be an angel at home? At church?**

My Angel Provides for Me

Halos for Little Angels

Elijah's Tree

Someone was sleeping, sleeping, sleeping.

Someone was sleeping,

Do you know who it was?

yell: Yes, Elijah!

Someone was bringing food, bringing food, bringing food.

Someone was bringing food,

Do you know who it was?

yell: Yes, an angel!

Someone sent the angel, sent the angel, sent the angel.

Someone sent the angel,

Do you know who it was?

yell: Yes, God! He provides for us.

Materials
- green paper
- tape
- scissors

Directions
1. Show how to loosely roll three sheets of paper together lengthwise into a tube and tape the outer sheet to secure.
2. Allow the students to use scissors to cut slits 1" apart and 4" down, all the way around the tube.
3. Show how to gently pull up on an inside fringe, until the branches of a tree appear.
4. Have the students wave their "trees" as they sing the song to the tune of "Do You Know the Muffin Man?"

My Angel Provides for Me

puzzle

· · · · · · · · · · ·

Materials
•puzzle, duplicated
•pencils

Usage

Encourage your group's math skills and help them learn the an important Bible verse with this puzzle. Younger children will need assistance with the addition— you may want to provide a small chart to help them along and avoid frustration.

All Our Needs

Add up all your needs. God can provide them all!
Add the numbers in the puzzle below
and find out what the Bible tells us.

(Clue: A=1, B=2, Y=25, Z=26)

___ ___   ___ ___ ___   ___ ___ ___ ___
6+7 20+5   3+4 10+5 2+2   20+3 5+4 6+6 3+9

___ ___ ___ ___   ___ ___ ___
9+4 2+3 1+4 10+10 1+0 10+2 7+5

___ ___ ___ ___   ___ ___ ___ ___ ___
22+3 7+8 20+1 9+9 7+7 2+3 5+0 1+3 7+12   according

___ ___   ___ ___ ___
18+2 1+14 2+6 2+7 2+17

___ ___ ___ ___ ___ ___ ___
3+4 7+5 10+5 9+9 8+1 7+8 18+3 4+15

___ ___ ___ ___ ___ ___   ___ ___
9+9 3+6 2+1 3+5 2+3 6+13   2+7 4+10

___ ___ ___ ___ ___ ___   ___ ___ ___ ___ ___
3+0 2+6 17+1 7+2 16+3 10+10 4+6 3+2 19+0 10+11 7+12

— Philippians 4:19

Solution is on page 96.

My Angel
Provides for Me

Surprise No-Bake Cakes

Materials
- recipe, duplicated
- 8 oz. peanut butter
- 2 T. honey
- ½ cup non-fat pow-dered milk
- raisins, nuts, carobs

Directions
1. Have the students help you put pea-nut butter, honey and dry milk in a bowl. Mix.
2. After mixing, place the dough on the table and knead it. If the dough be-comes sticky, add more dry milk.
3. Form the dough into small cakes.
4. Let the students help you to choose the surprise ingre-dient for the middle (raisins, nuts, chips, etc.).
5. Poke a hole with your finger in the middle of the cake, hide the surprise and roll the cake in your hand to form a ball.
6. Distribute recipes to take home.

Recipe for Surprise No-Bake Cakes

- 8 oz. peanut butter
- 2 T. honey
- ½ cup non-fat powdered milk
- raisins, nuts, carobs

Mix peanut butter, honey and dry milk together. Use extra dry milk if dough becomes too sticky. Form into small cakes, then place a surprise inside and roll into a ball. Read 1 Kings 19:7-8 or have someone read it to you, then eat your cake and see how much strength you gain, like Elijah.

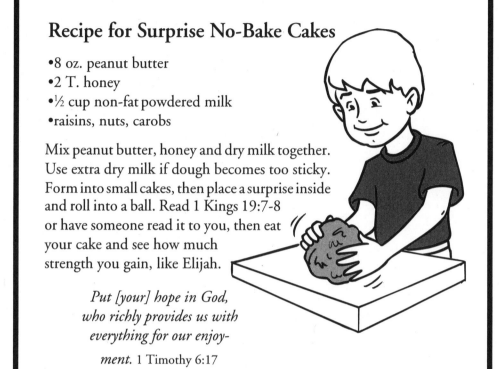

Put [your] hope in God, who richly provides us with everything for our enjoy-ment. 1 Timothy 6:17

Discuss
Read 1 Kings 19:7-8 to the class. Say, **The cakes the angel fed Elijah had a surprise ingredient. With the strength he received from the cakes he traveled 40 days and nights. Let's make some Surprise Cakes to see how much strength our "surprise" gives us.**

My Angel Provides for Me

61

Act It Out

skit

Usage

Many children learn effectively through active tools, like skits. Photocopy the script so everyone can follow along. Repeat the skit as many times as the children desire to allow everyone a chance to play a role.

Setting:	A tree in the desert. three children bunched together, arms raised and swaying
Characters:	Elijah angel
Props:	flask of water small cakes
Narrator:	Elijah had been running for his life. Jezebel was angry with him and said he would be dead within 24 hours. Elijah was so tired from running away that he lay down under a tree.

Elijah enters. He throws himself down under the "tree."

Elijah:	I've had enough, Lord. Take my life. *he falls asleep*
Angel:	Get up and eat. *places water and cakes by Elijah's head*
Elijah:	*sits up, eats cake and drinks water, then goes back to sleep*
Angel:	Get up and eat. *places more water and cakes by his head*
Elijah:	Thank You, God, for sending an angel to provide for me.

A Handsome Tree

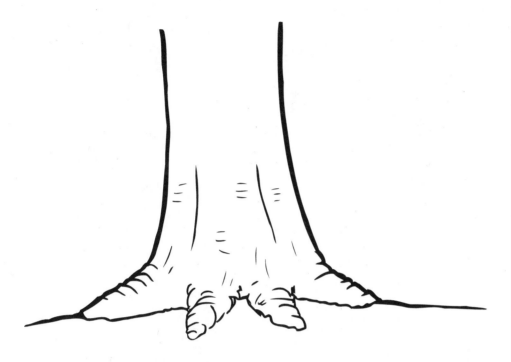

Materials
- tree trunk, duplicated
- green construction paper
- glue
- brown crayons
- scissors

Directions
1. Have the students color and cut out the tree trunk.
2. Show how they can spread their fingers and trace their left hand on the green construction paper. Paper should be turned horizontal.
3. Then have them place their right thumb on the left one just traced and carefully trace that hand onto the paper (using opposite hands is fun!).
4. Next, they should place their left palm in the middle of the finger drawing and trace it.
5. After tracing, have them cut out their "branches" and glue to the trunk.

My Angel Provides for Me

Variation
Make a large trunk (you may enlarge the trunk above) and hang it on the wall. Blindfold each child. As you turn the child around four times say, "God provides for (name) ." Let the children try to post their branches to the right spot on the trunk, similar to "Pin the Tail on the Donkey."

Discuss
Say, **Elijah was sleeping under a tree when God sent an angel to feed him. God always provides what we need. He's always watching; He never sleeps. When has He provided for you?**

puzzle

• • • • • • • • • • • •

Materials
• puzzle, duplicated
• pencils

Usage
Children may become confused with the unusual names and situations in the Bible. Use this quick puzzle to help them identify the main characters in this lesson's Bible story.

Which One Is Right?

Finish the sentence by circling the correct answer.

I am the queen. I am angry with Elijah.

I am running from the queen. I am so tired I wish I could die.

I ran with Elijah as far as Beersheba.

I sent an angel to provide for tired Elijah.

I woke Elijah and fed him cakes and water.

My Angel Provides for Me

Solution is on page 96.

64

Running Elijah Finger Puppets

craft

Story Script

1. Jezebel is angry.
   Come, come, come.
   Hurry, hurry, servant,
   We've got to run, run, run.
2. My sandals are saying,
   "Slap, slap, slap."
   I'm so tired of running,
   let me take a nap.
3. Fly, Fly, Fly,
   the angel God sent came fast.
   Yum, Yum, Yum,
   I have food at last.

Materials

• finger puppets and script, duplicated
• crayons
• scissors

Directions

1. Have the class color and carefully cut out the finger puppets.
2. Show how to cut out the finger holes.
3. Instruct the students to poke their fingers through the holes and take turns telling the story to those seated next to them, using the script or their own versions.

My Angel Provides for Me

65

Chapter 7
My Angel Comforts Me

Memory Verse

The Lord has comforted his people. Isaiah 52:9

Story to Share
The Angels Comfort Jesus

Jesus wanted to be alone with His Heavenly Father, God, so He went by Himself to the wilderness to pray. Jesus spent 40 days there praying to God. During those days He didn't want anything to distract Him from His communion with God so He did not eat. At the end of the 40 days Jesus was exhausted and very hungry.

All of a sudden, Jesus realized He wasn't alone. Turning around, He saw Satan. "What are you doing here?" asked Jesus.

Satan was angry because he knew God had plans for Jesus. God wanted to provide sinful people with a way to have their sins forgiven. In order to do that, a perfect, sinless person had to die, so God sent His Son, Jesus, to the world to be that person. Jesus had power that came from God. Satan wanted Him to use that power in a wrong way. So he tempted Jesus.

"It's been a long time since You've eaten, Jesus. If You are truly the Son of God, why don't You turn these stones into bread so You can have something to eat?"

Jesus was hungry, but He said to Satan, "It is written, 'Man does not live on bread alone, but on every word that comes from the mouth of God.' Listening to God and doing what He says is more important than food for my hunger."

Instead of leaving Jesus alone, Satan took Him to the edge of the temple roof, 400 feet off the ground. "Jump to the ground, Jesus," said Satan. "If your Father really loves You, He will send angels to carry You to the ground."

Quietly, Jesus answered, "It is written that you should not test God."

Satan was really angry now. He took Him to the top of a high place. "Look at all these kingdoms. Just bow down and worship me, and I will give You all You see."

"It is written, 'Worship the Lord your God, and serve Him only.' It is God alone that I worship," said Jesus. "Now go away. I will not do what you want. I will only do what My Father in Heaven wants Me to do."

Satan left, knowing he was defeated. Jesus was alone once again, but not for long. He heard the swishing of wings and looked up. There, in the sky, were angels coming to take care of Jesus. God had sent His angels to bring food and comfort to Jesus.

— based on Matthew 4:1-11

Questions for Discussion

1. Have you ever had someone you love die?
2. Who cares when these things happen to us?

• • • • • • • • • •

Materials
•puzzle, duplicated
•pencils

Discuss
Say, When you receive Jesus into your heart, the devil is angry. He will do all he can to keep you from doing what God wants you to do. He will tempt you to be unkind, to lie, to swear and many other things. When Satan comes to you, do what Jesus did. Fight back with Scripture. Here's a verse to help you. Say, "No, Satan, God doesn't want me to even think about doing those things." Then do what this verse says.

Victory Over Temptation

Fill in the blanks with the words below.

right   admirable
lovely   pure
noble   true

Whatever is ___ ___ u ___ , whatever is ___ ___ b ___ ___ ,

whatever is ___ ___ ___ h ___ , whatever is ___ u ___ ___ ,

whatever is ___ ___ v ___ ___ ___ , whatever is

___ d ___ ___ ___ ___ ___ ___ ___ — if anything is excellent or

praiseworthy — think about such things.

— Philippians 4:8

Solution is on page 96.

Angel Lace-up

craft

. . . .

Materials
- angel patterns, duplicated on heavy white paper
- crayons or markers
- scissors
- yarn or string (taped ends)
- hole punch

Directions
1. Have the class color, cut out and glue the angels together, right side out. Allow to dry.
2. Show how to make holes at the dots using the hole punch.
3. Starting at the top, show how to thread the string down through one hole and up through the next.
4. Help the students tie a bow with the leftover string at the top back.

The Lord has comforted his people.
Isaiah 52:9

My Angel Comforts Me

puzzle

• • • • • • • • • • • • •

Materials
•puzzle, duplicated
•pencils
•crayons

Usage
To reinforce the lesson's Bible story, have the class do this puzzle just before the end of your session. Allow them to color the picture and take the sheet home as a reminder for them (and their parents) of the day's theme.

My Angel Comforts Me

Mixed-up Story

Unscramble the words to finish the story.

Jesus went to the wilderness to_____ . He was there ____ days.

rypa   rotfy

During this time He did not _____ . Satan came to _____

tea   mettp

Jesus. He wanted Jesus to_____ . Satan tempted Jesus to turn

ins

the _____ into bread. He tempted Jesus to jump off the highest

srcok

point of the_____ . And he tempted Jesus to bow down and

meltpe

_____ him. Jesus did not sin. He said, "Get _____ from me,

pwiorhs   yawa

Satan." God sent _____ to comfort Jesus with food and love.

gaensl

Solution is on page 96.

A Lesson from Jesus

puzzle

· · · · · · · · · · · ·

Let away from me, Satan!

_____ _____ _____

_____ _____

Materials
- puzzle, duplicated
- mirror
- pencils

Directions
1. Pass around a mirror and have the students hold the paper up to it to read the message.
2. Instruct them to quietly write it in the spaces below.
3. After all have finished, read the phrase together aloud.

Discuss
Say, **Jesus knew the secret to not giving in to temptation. You can use these same five words when Satan tempts you to do wrong.**

My Angel Comforts Me

Angel Twins

puzzle

Materials
•puzzle, duplicated
•crayons

Directions
1. Instruct the students to work on their own to find the three sets of twins.
2. Have them color each set the same color.

Discuss
Say, God sent angels to comfort Jesus when he was tired, hungry and sad. Are there times when you are sad? God will comfort you, too.

Are You Tempted?

song

Are you tempted?

Are you tempted?

To do wrong?

To do wrong?

Tell the mean, old devil,

To get away from you.

Use God's Word.

Use God's Word.

Are you sad?

Are you sad?

Tired and alone?

Tired and alone?

God will send your angel,

With comfort and joy.

He loves you.

He loves you.

Directions

Sing to the tune of "Are You Sleeping?" The children will catch on to this song quickly because of the familiar tune. Make up your own verses to extend it, or allow the children to suggest their own words.

My Angel Comforts Me

craft

Comforted With Love

Materials
- hearts, duplicated
- pink or red construction paper
- scissors
- magnet bits
- glue

Directions
1. Have the students cut out both hearts.
2. Show how to trace the large heart onto construction paper and cut out.
3. The small heart should be glued to the center of the larger heart.
4. Give each child a magnet bit to glue to the back of the heart.
5. Say, **Give the heart to someone who is sad. It will remind them of God's comfort.**

My Angel Comforts Me

Halo Treats

How to Make Halo Treats

What You Need:
- bread
- peanut butter
- raisins, carob chips or sunflower seeds
- doughnut cutter
- plastic knife

What to Do:
Cut your bread with the doughnut cutter. Top with peanut butter and your choice of decorations. You can also make Halo Treats using bagels and spreadable cheese or cream cheese, plus olives, pepperoni or celery. Be creative and design your own halo — you are a unique angel!

The Lord has comforted his people.
Isaiah 52:9

Materials
- recipe, duplicated
- bread
- peanut butter
- raisins, carob chips and sunflower seeds
- doughnut cutters
- plastic knives

Directions
1. Show how to use the doughnut cutter to cut halos from bread.
2. Allow the students to use plastic knives to spread peanut butter on the halos.
3. Place raisins, carob chips and sunflower seeds in bowls so the children may decorate their halos.
4. Distribute duplicated instructions for the children to make Halo Treats at home.

Variation
Use spreadable cheese and top with chopped olives, pepperoni or celery. Bagels may also be used for bread.

My Angel Comforts Me

Another Snack Idea...
Heavenly Treats

Materials
- angel food cake
- toothpicks
- chocolate syrup
- whipped topping
- strawberry topping
- condiment cups

Directions
1. Cut angel food cake into cubes.
2. Stick a toothpick in each one.
3. Fill condiment cups with toppings of your choice.
4. Dip cake in toppings.

Chapter 8
My Angel Praises God

Memory Verse

Let everything that has breath praise the Lord. Praise the Lord.
Psalm 150:6

Story to Share
A Week's Work

A long time ago there was nothing. No people. No animals. No plants. No Earth! There was nothing except God and His angels. But God wanted a world where people and animals and plants could live. So God created the heavens and the earth.

All was dark, so God said, "Let there be light." That's all it took, just God saying, "Let there be light," and suddenly light appeared. God took the light part and called it "day." The dark part He called "night." God did all of this in one day.

On the second day of creation, God made the sky. The third day God made the sea and dry land. When God made the land, plants and grass and flowers and trees grew. God made the land beautiful.

Then God wanted lights in the sky. He wanted a large light to shine over the day and a small light to shine at night. So, on the fourth day, God made the sun and moon. God put stars to shine around the moon.

Also on the fourth day, God created animals in the sea – all of the fish and whales and dolphins! Then He made birds to fly around the air and nest in the trees.

God used the fifth day to make land animals. He made a big animal with humps on its back: a camel. He made a tiny animal that has a round, fluffy tail and hops: a rabbit. He made an animal that moos and gives us milk: a cow. And He made a big, gray animal with huge ears and a long nose: an elephant. He made everything from the swinging monkeys to the giraffe with its long neck.

After all of the things God had made, there were still no people on the earth. God wanted to make someone like Himself, so He made a man and a woman: Adam and Eve.

God looked at everything He made and He was so happy! He was pleased with His own work. God's angels were pleased with what He made, also. They shouted for joy and praised God.

This was all done in six days. God took the last day of the week to rest. His work was complete. He rested and listened to the angels praise His name.

— based on Genesis 1–2; Job 38:4-7

Questions for Discussion

1. What can we learn from the angels in this story?
2. For what can we praise God?

puzzle

· · · · · · · · · · ·

Materials
•puzzle, duplicated
•pencils

Usage
Your class may be confused about this lesson's memory verse because of the repeated "praise the Lord" phrase. Help them to understand the emphasis by giving the second "praise the Lord" a more exclamatory sound when you say the verse.

Angels and Hearts

Three words are missing from the memory verse.
Unscramble the words on the angels below
and write them in the correct space.
Each word is used twice.

Let everything that has breath _____ _____

_____. _____ _____

_____. Psalm 150:6

eth oLdr

eriaps

Solution is on page 96.

· ·

Praising the Lord puts joy in our hearts. In the hearts
below, write something for which you can praise the
Lord, then draw a smile on your face.

78

Creative Animals

craft

· · · · · · · · · · ·

Materials
- animals, duplicated
- crayons
- scissors
- glue

Directions
1. Have the class color and cut out the animal parts.
2. Instruct the students to close their eyes and mix up the parts, then to try to put the animals together. Ask, **What do they look like? What if God had created them that way?**
3. Then allow the students to glue the animals together "like God created them." Ask, **Isn't God's way best?**

Discuss
Say, God knew what He was doing when He made animals. What if monkeys had elephant ears? What if turtles had long necks like giraffes? They couldn't get them under their shell very well, could they?

My Angel Praises God

I Praise Him, Too

Angels praise God for the birds,

flap arms like bird flying

For the birds, for the birds.

Angels praise God for the birds.

I praise Him, too.

Directions

Sing to the tune of "London Bridge Is Falling Down." Allow the children to pick an animal for which to thank God. Fit the animal in the song with the appropriate action.

Angels praise God for the sun,

hold hands in circle above head

For the sun, for the sun.

Angels praise God for the sun.

I praise Him, too.

Angels praise God for the stars,

wiggle fingers like twinkling stars

For the stars, for the stars.

Angels praise God for the stars.

I praise Him, too.

Angels praise God for the ducks,

squat down and waddle like a duck

For the ducks, for the ducks.

Angels praise God for the ducks.

I praise Him, too.

**My Angel
Praises God**

Instruments of Praise

In Psalm 150 we are told to praise God with many instruments. Read the chapter and see who can write the instruments first. The first letter is written to get you started.

1. T _ _ _ _ _ _ _

2. H _ _ _

3. L _ _ _

4. T _ _ _ _ _ _ _ _ _

5. S _ _ _ _ _ _

6. F _ _ _ _

7. C _ _ _ _ _ _

Solution is on page 96.

Praiseful Strings

Sometimes we call our hands our "instruments of 10 strings." Join hands to form a circle. One person stands in the middle. Everyone claps hands and chants, "Praise-God-Praise-God-I-Praise-God-for..." The one in the middle points to someone and that person must clap his hands above his head and says what he praises God for. That person is then in the middle and points to someone else. Continue until everyone has had a turn.

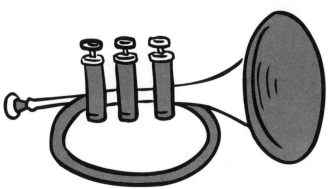

puzzle/game

Materials
•puzzle, duplicated
•pencils
•Bibles

Usage
You may read Psalm 150 to younger children. Older students may read the chapter and complete the puzzle themselves. If you have access to any of the instruments listed (even toy versions) bring them in and demonstrate how they sound.

My Angel Praises God

craft

Materials

- book, duplicated
- colored pencils or markers
- scissors
- optional: star and animal stickers

Directions

1. Have the class cut out the book on the solid lines.
2. Show how to fold the paper in half and then in quarters at the dashed lines.
3. Instruct the students to draw mini illustrations of what God created above each day.
3. On the front of the book, help the children write their names on the line.
4. If desired, allow the students to select some stickers for their books.

My Angel Praises God

The First Seven Days

DAY 4

DAY 2

DAY 3

DAY 1

DAY 5

DAY 6

ON DAY 7, GOD RESTED!

Praises God for Creation.

Secret Message

Who should praise the Lord?
The angels do.
Who else should?
Color all the boxes below with words and dots in them.
Then write the words in the uncolored boxes on the lines below.

puzzle

Materials
•puzzle, duplicated
•pencils
•crayons

Usage
Kids love secret messages and codes. Provide crayons for coloring the boxes and pencils to write the words on the lines.

• David	• Kaitlin	Everyone
• Joshua	• Amanda	that
• Justin	hath	• Bryce
• Emily	breath	• Christie

_____ _____ _____

_____ praise the Lord. Praise the Lord.

Does that include you? _____

Solution is on page 96.

My Angel Praises God

83

People of Praise

In the Bible, there are many people who praised God.
Learn who they are by reading the Scriptures and filling in the spaces.
Some are individuals and others are groups of people.

Materials
•puzzle, duplicated
•pencils
•Bibles

Usage

Be sure each child has a Bible in which to look up the verses. Help younger children find the verses.

Acts 16:25

P __ __ __

Luke 1:67-68

__ __ __ __ __ R __ __ __

2 Chronicles 20:20-22

__ __ __ A __

Matthew 21:15-16

__ __ I __ __ __ __

Luke 2:20

S __ __ __ __ __ __ __

Luke 2:13-14

__ __ __ E __ __ __

When should we praise God? Add it up and find the answer!

2=O, 4=N, 6=A, 8=G, 10=L, 12=D, 14=Y

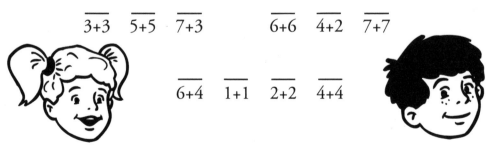

$$\overline{3+3} \quad \overline{5+5} \quad \overline{7+3} \qquad \overline{6+6} \quad \overline{4+2} \quad \overline{7+7}$$

$$\overline{6+4} \quad \overline{1+1} \quad \overline{2+2} \quad \overline{4+4}$$

Check your answer by looking up Psalm 35:28.

Praise All Week

Friday

Spread peanut butter on animal crackers. Gather your stuffed animals together and have a party. Thank God for making all the animals!

Tuesday

Eat some marshmallows and imagine they are clouds. Look at the sky and see if you can find some animal-shaped clouds. Thank God for the sky!

Sunday

Rest, just like God did. And join the angels in praising God for all He has done!

Saturday

Draw your family. Cut each one out and glue to a popsicle stick. Thank God for all the people He has made —including you!

Monday

Find a piece of black construction paper. Trace around a plate to make a circle and cut out. Using a white crayon, write the word LIGHT on the dark circle. Thank God for making the world!

Thursday

Place a peach half on your plate. Poke toothpicks around the edge for the sun's rays. Thank God for the sun, moon and stars!

Wednesday

Spoon dirt into a resealable plastic sandwich bag. Add a tablespoon of water and a few popcorn kernels. Seal the bag and hang in a sunny window. Your kernels will begin to sprout in about a week. Thank God for the plants, grass, flowers and trees!

Secret Password Hint
Pr__ __s__ th__ L__rd.

Solution is on page 96.

activity

• • • • • • • • • • • •

Directions

Duplicate this page as either a take-home sheet or an in-class activity if your group meets every day of the week. Or, do one day's activity with the class then send the sheet home. Children are to color in each day's shape as they remember to praise God. The daily activities are optional. Younger children may need adult assistance to read the activities. If you send the sheet home, tell your class to bring it back the next week with the secret password written on back. A hint is included at the bottom of the page. Tell them they must figure out the password on their own.

My Angel Praises God

Chapter 9
Miscellaneous Angelic Activities

What Has Your Angel Been Doing?

Dear Parent,

_____

_____

_____

_____

_____

_____

_____

_____

_____

_____

Thank you for bringing your angel to class!

_____

Supply Help

teacher help

Directions

Duplicate and distribute the note. Check off the items you need and insert the date on the blank line when you want them brought in. You may issue one note at the beginning of the eight lessons or issue one note per week or every few weeks, depending on your needs.

Dear Friend,

We are learning about God's angels. There are a few items we could use to complete the activities in our lessons. I have checked off those that we need on _____.

❏ bread
❏ envelopes, letter-size
❏ cake, angel food
❏ carob chips
❏ craft sticks
❏ doughnut cutters
❏ fabric, white
❏ honey
❏ ice cream toppings
❏ lollipops
❏ nail polish, clear
❏ newspapers, old
❏ paint brushes
❏ paint smocks
❏ paper fasteners

❏ paper lunch sacks
❏ paper plates, 9"
❏ peanut butter
❏ plastic drinking straws
❏ potato peelers
❏ powdered milk, non-fat
❏ raisins
❏ self-stick plastic, clear
❏ small photo of your child
❏ string
❏ sunflower seeds
❏ toothpicks
❏ waxed paper
❏ yarn

Thank you for your help!

_____

God Gave Me an Angel

Angel Mobile

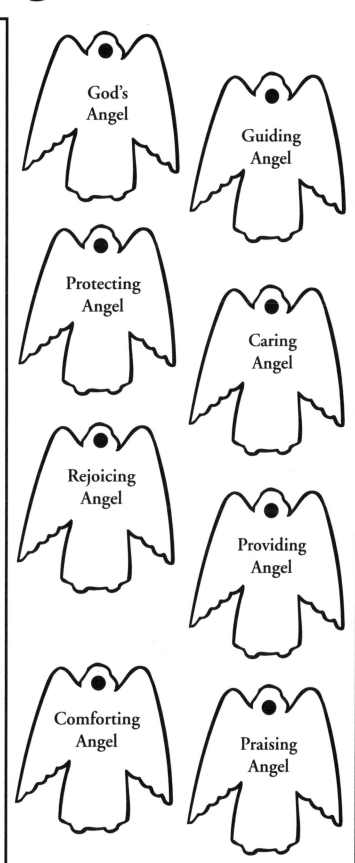

An Angel for Me _____

God's Angel

Guiding Angel

Protecting Angel

Caring Angel

Rejoicing Angel

Providing Angel

Comforting Angel

Praising Angel

activity

• • • • • • • • • • •

Usage
Encourage and reward verse memorization with this simple mobile that you can hang from your classroom ceiling or on a bulletin board. Each child should make a mobile at the beginning of the eight sessions.

Materials
• angels and bar, duplicated to heavy paper
• crayons
• scissors
• string or yarn
• hole punch

Directions
1. Have the class color and cut out the angels and the bar.
2. Each child should write his or her name on the line.
3. Punch holes at the dots. As the students memorize the verses, hang the angels on the bar with string. Tie string at the top for hanging.

God Gave Me an Angel

I Will Be an Angel

activity

Directions
Duplicate and fill in as desired.

Usage
Use as an incentive for:
• learning memory verses
• maintaining quiet during the lesson
• promoting good sharing habits

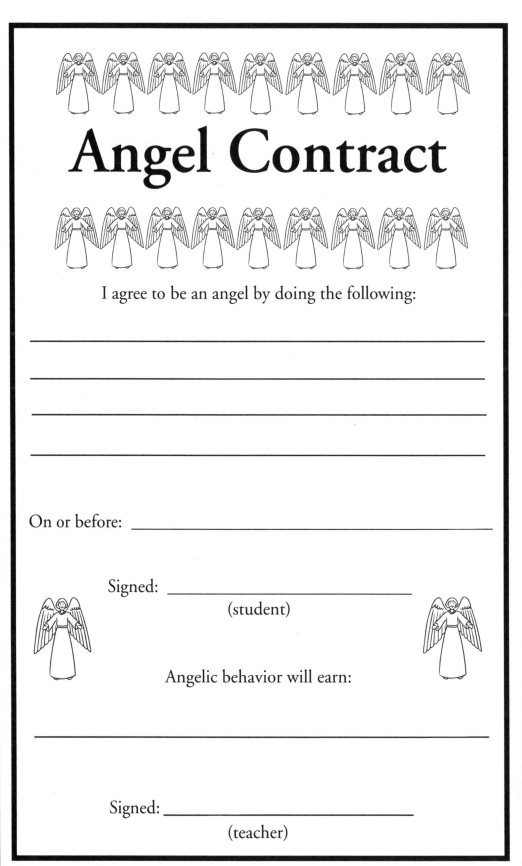

Angel Contract

I agree to be an angel by doing the following:

_____

_____

_____

_____

On or before: _____

Signed: _____
(student)

Angelic behavior will earn:

_____

Signed: _____
(teacher)

Angel Puppet

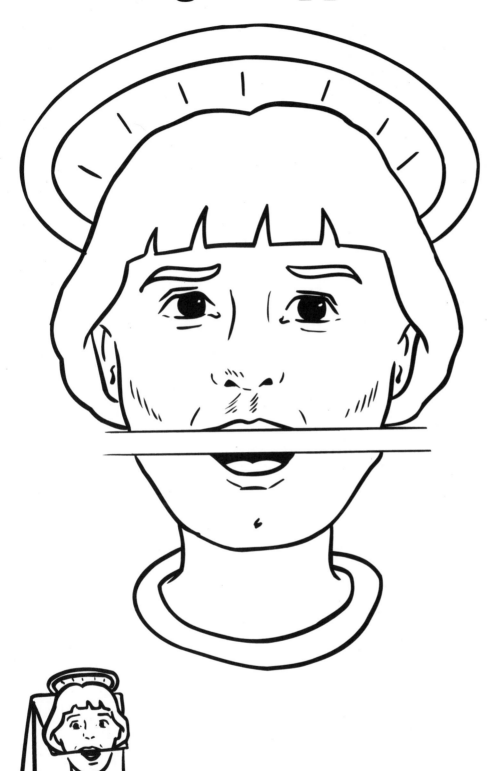

Usage

Introduce the memory verse with an angel puppet, or let the students make their own.

Materials

• angel, duplicated
• crayons
• scissors
• lunch bag
• glue

Directions

1. Have the students color and cut out the angel face.
2. Show how to glue the face to the lunch bag, as shown in the bottom illustration.
3. Tell the students they may use their angel puppets to help them say the memory verse.

God Gave Me an Angel

Good Behavior Headband

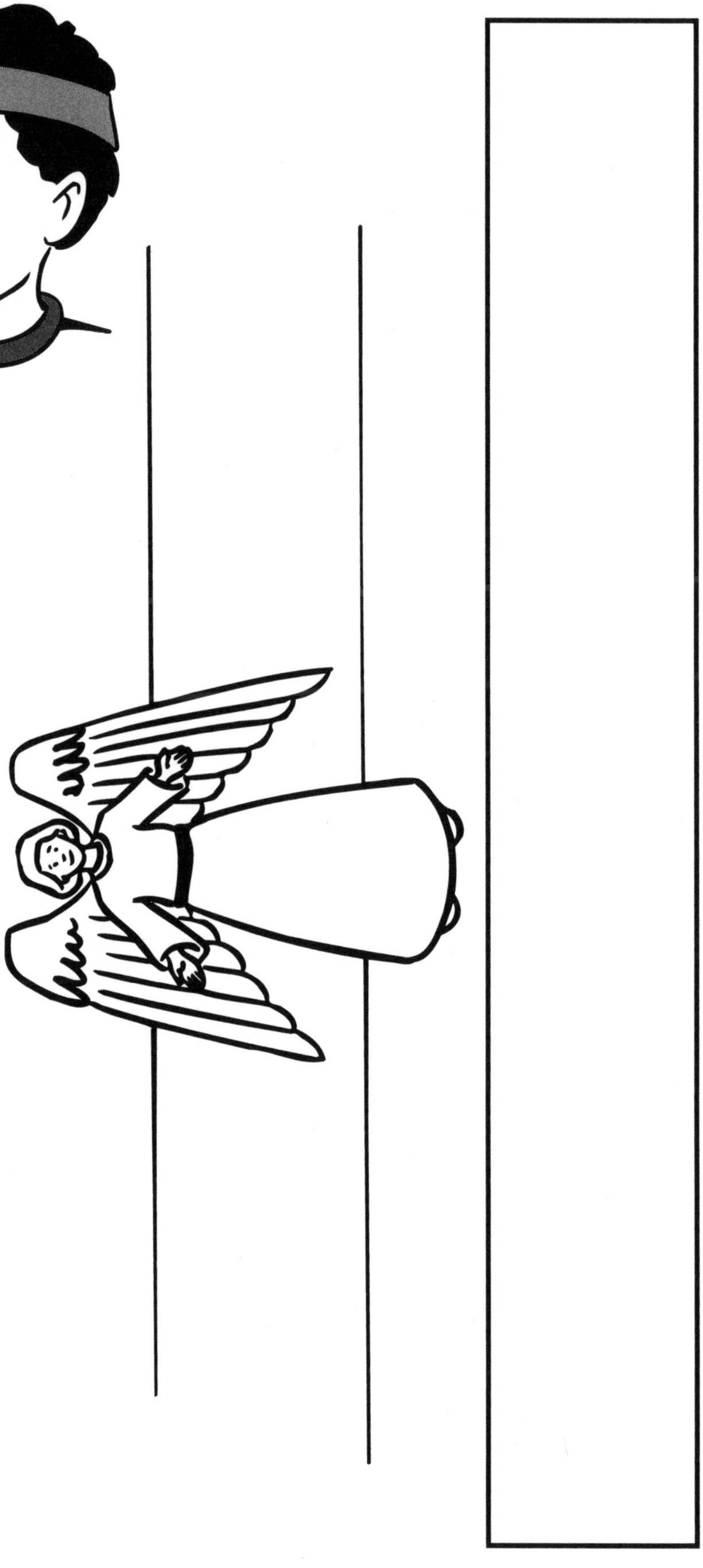

Usage

Award and encourage listening, sharing, participation, etc.

Materials

- headband pieces, duplicated
- crayons
- scissors
- stapler or glue
- tape (if using stapler)

Directions

1. Have the students color and cut out the bands.
2. Show how they can size the headband by stapling or gluing the plain band to the front until it fits. If you use a stapler, be sure to cover the staples with tape to prevent scratching.

Wiggle Buster
for Little Angels

game

• • • • • • • • • • •

1. Angels are standing tall.

   stand at attention

Usage

When your younger students have difficulty paying attention to the lesson, try this fun learning activity. Call out each movement. After the children learn the movements, say them faster and faster.

2. Angels listen for God's commands.

   cup left ear, bend to opposite shoulder, repeat with right ear

3. When God commands, angels say, "Yes."

   nod head vigoursly

4. Off they fly to obey.

   move arms up and down

5. Soon they're back, bowing low.

   bow low, ending sitting on floor

**God Gave Me
an Angel**

Angels from Our Class

Materials
- angel, duplicated to heavy paper
- photo of each child
- scissors
- glue

Directions
1. Cut out the angels' faces. Glue the children's pictures to the backs.
2. Let the students fill in the blanks.
3. Post the angels on the bulletin board.
4. Cut large lettering that reads: AN-GELS FROM OUR CLASS.
5. If you have additional space on the board, display completed angel crafts and puzzles.

God Gave Me an Angel

My Favorite

Snack: _____

Color: _____

Song: _____

Book: _____

Holiday: _____

Activity: _____

Rubber Stamp Angels

. . . .

Materials

- flat piece of rubber inner tube (or shoe insoles)
- scissors
- heavy-duty glue
- small wood blocks (or small boxes, spools or film canisters)

Directions

1. Trace the outline of an angel on flat pieces of inner tube.
2. Cut out the angel shapes and glue to wood blocks. Let glue dry 24 hours.
3. To make individual stamp pads, place a folded paper towel in a shallow container and pour in a small amount of tempera paint.

What Can I Do With Stamps?

There are a lot of creative things you can do with your new stamps:

Stained Glass Creations — Place a piece of white paper under colored cellophane (so the design can be easily seen). Let the children stamp angels on the cellophane. When the ink has dried, tape the cellophane to a window.

Take-home Treat Bags — Have the children stamp angels on a brown or white lunch sack.

Personalized Placemats — Have the children stamp a border of angels on an 8 ½" x 11" piece of heavy paper. Write their names in the middle. Cover with clear, self-stick paper.

Room Decorations — Cut a light-colored streamer into 6-foot lengths. Have the children stamp angels on the streamers. Let them help you hang the streamers to give your classroom an angelic atmosphere.

God Gave Me an Angel

Answers to Puzzles

Memory Verse Rebus, page 13
See that you do not look down of one of these little ones. For I tell you that their angels in heaven always see the face of my Father in heaven.
— Matthew 18:10

Missing Os and Es, page 14
See that you do not look down of one of these little ones. For I tell you that their angels in heaven always see the face of my Father in heaven.
— Matthew 18:10

Hiding Angels, page 19
Number of angels = 10

Heaven Rejoices, page 22
Down words: persons
               sinner
               heaven
Across words: repents
               ninety
               rejoicing

A Surprise Word, page 24
harp, wings, sing, heaven, halo, trumpets, Angels

Star Pupils, page 25
Who was Jesus' mother? Mary
Who was Jesus' earthly father? Joseph
Where was Jesus born? In a stable
Who were watching their sheep? Shepherds
Who came to tell them Jesus was born? Angels
What do angels do when our sins are forgiven? Rejoice

The Most Important Thing, page 29
Angels obey God.

Standing Guard, page 32

Broken Chains, page 33
1. He was chained to two guards.
2. sleeping
3. struck him on the side.
4. it opened by itself
5. the house of Mary

6. praying
7. Rhoda
8. no, they thought it was an angel
9. they were astonished
10. God will guide me, too.

Afraid? Trust in God, page 42
When I am afraid, I will trust in you.

Bible Verse Protection, page 44
1. ENCAMPS
2. FEATHERS
3. MOUTHS
4. SHELTER
5. PEOPLE
6. CALL
7. DON'T
8. CONCERNING
9. SPARROWS
10. NUMBERED

Memory Verse Puzzle, page 51
I am the Lord…I am with you and will watch over you wherever you go. Genesis 28:15

A Pillow? page 53
ROCK

All Our Needs, page 60
My God will meet all your needs according to his glorious riches in Christ Jesus.

Which One is Right? page 64
Jezebel, Elijah, Servant, God, Angel

Victory Over Temptation, page 68
true, noble, right, pure, lovely, admirable

Mixed-Up Story, page 70
pray, forty, eat, tempt, sin, rocks, temple, worship, away, angels

A Lesson from Jesus, page 71
Get away from me, Satan!

Memory Verse, page 78
Praise the Lord, Praise the Lord.

Instruments of Praise, page 81
trumpet, harp, lyre, tambourine, strings, flute, cymbals

Secret Message, page 83
Everyone that hath breath; yes

People of Praise, page 84
Paul, Zechariah, Judah, children, shepherds, angels all the time.

Praise All Week, page 85
Praise the Lord